MW00777293

When I moved internationally for the third time, I felt so alone and misunderstood. Even though I have lived abroad for well over a decade, these liturgies were exactly what I needed and brought me to tears with every sentence. For any stage of life, each liturgy has something to say to those of us struggling to put words to our feelings. It has freed my heart to be able to pray through these and know someone else has felt the same as I!

Caitlin Lieder
16 years in Germany and England

This book helped give words to my prayers. It made me feel seen, known, and understood. It's the perfect prayer book for anyone who lives abroad, is thinking about living abroad, or loves someone who lives abroad.

Clare
2 years in Lebanon

For those who live between two worlds, having the somewhat unique opportunity to experience the joys and hardships of being not fully at home in either one—this book, and all it holds, is an absolute TREASURE. The writers have beautifully crafted words in the form of prayers, for moments when we have none. Somehow they have put onto paper the very pieces of my heart that I myself am unable to express. I know I will return to these pages again and again in prayer for months and years to come.

Tina Skinner
7 years in Indonesia

As an expat, I have often felt lost and alone, but reading this book helped me to feel known and helped me put into words all of the emotions stirring deep in my soul. Best of all, these prayers point me to Christ – the Foundation and Surety of our lives. Read these slowly, savor the words of encouragement, and pray the prayers out loud. I will be returning to these again and again!

Claire K.
4 years in East Asia and Taiwan

As a Christ follower who is not currently serving Him overseas, I found this book not only beautiful, but immensely helpful. It has given me a deeper insight into hardships, longings, joys, and sorrows experienced by those living outside their own culture. It will help to form my prayers for them and those they are serving.

Rachel Crosby
A close friend of several expat families

This book should be given to every new worker at their pre-field orientation. It gives words to so many things we all experience day after day while living and serving cross-culturally. Whether you are a rookie or a veteran worker, this book will be a blessing!

Matthew Wright
ATCK and Member Care provider, 20+ years in Albania, Australia, and Greece

There is a unique loneliness that can happen in the life of an expat. In this beautiful collection of prayers, those who are living outside of their passport country will be reminded that they are not alone in the struggles that come with this life. Not only will the reader be comforted by the authors who have "been there," but these pages will help them draw near to the One in whom home is truly found.

Becca B.
5 years in Europe

Liturgies and Laments of the Sojourner: Volume 1 will soon be on the night stand or in the handbag of every global worker. These rich prayers take the events of daily life in a foreign setting—packing, unpacking, shopping, traffic, loss of electricity—and transform them into holy communion with Jesus, turning our eyes from the chaos of cultures to the Creator of them.

Eva Burkholder
30 combined years in Papua New Guinea (as a TCK) and Indonesia (for work)

Honest, real, beautiful encouragement from fellow sojourners – these liturgies give words to my heart when I'm too tired or overwhelmed to know what to pray. Reading them washes truth over my soul and feels like a friend praying for me, orienting my heart towards the character of God and my eyes toward eternity.

Lindsay Campbell
2 years Switzerland and Côte d'Ivoire

These liturgies speak to the heart of so many experiences where I failed to have words to express the depth of the emotions. This is a handbook of prayers and felt experiences, a place of belonging for those of us who feel like we don't always have a space. Thank you ladies, for the heart and tears you have poured into this work, and the ways these words bind us as we sojourn together in the places we have been set down.

Karyn M.
6.5 years in Chiang Mai, Thailand

Similar to the Holy Spirit's intercession on our behalf when we don't know what to pray, *Liturgies and Laments of the Sojourner: Volume 1* gives voice to the deepest, most personal experiences that unite expats around the globe and across generations. Whether you're feeling stifled in your attempts to articulate your own cross-cultural (mis)adventures, wrestling to find words to encourage a friend or family member living abroad, or have simply stumbled across this resource in your own journey to the nations, you have not found yourself pausing here by accident. Curl up with your coffee or tea, prayerfully thumb through these pages, and breathe deeply… inhale, then exhale.

Abby B.
1 year in East Asia

This volume is a friend that opens and anchors my heart to God. I found myself tearing up over words that resonated and moved my spirit heavenward. Our loved ones, organizations, and cross-cultural neighbors aren't always the ones we can share certain burdens with and that gets lonely. I'm grateful for this friend I can call on any time.

Jennifer PC
10 years in South Asia Indonesia

I believe this book is an invaluable resource for the Church and the sojourner. I found it a source of encouragement and direction of prayer for the many complexities that are hard to put into words while living cross culturally. It challenged me to take every little struggle and stressor to the Father throughout the day. I also believe this is a great resource for our passport country family members and churches to connect them to the daily struggles of the sojourner and know how to support them in prayer in the day to day.

Jessica Williamson
13 years in Kenya and Iraq

LITURGIES & LAMENTS FOR THE SOJOURNER

Volume One

VINEHOUSE
PUBLISHING, LLC.

To request permissions, contact the publisher at vinehousepublishing@gmail.com.

Paperback ISBN: 979-8-9878644-1-8

Ebook ISBN: 979-8-9878644-0-1

Library of Congress Control Number: 2023933178

First paperback edition March 2023.

Edited by Alicia Boyce and Heather Fallis

Cover design by Tamika Rybinski

Plane vector by Pixart

Layout by Tamika Rybinski

Vinehouse Publishing, LLC

400 Hubbert Dairy Rd.

Guin, AL 35563

TABLE OF CONTENTS

DEDICATION

We wrote these prayers for the ones who have suitcases which rarely collect dust.

We wrote these prayers for those who are regularly reminded they don't fit in.

We wrote these prayers for the adaptable, multilingual, lifelong learners.

We wrote these prayers for the sojourners who are carrying home in their heart.

While this global life comes with many joys and blessings, there's also something about this life that makes all our weaknesses rise to the surface. We regularly come face-to-face with our sins, flaws, and insufficiencies. That's why it's such good news that our weakness is an opportunity for Christ's power to be made perfect in us. We invite you to allow your weaknesses, doubts, frustrations, and worry to melt away in the presence of the Lord. The new to you is not new to God. He is already waiting for you in the places you've yet to arrive—whether that's a physical location on the map or the position of your heart.

These prayers are like modern day psalm—full of raw honesty and sincere emotions, yet bent on finding the "but You, O Lord" in all circumstances. May the warm light of the Lord pass on through these pages and spread to places all around the globe. And may you feel right at home, wherever you are, because you feel at home in the presence of Jesus.

Sojourning with you,

Alicia, Heather, and Tamika

HOW TO USE THIS BOOK

In this life of sojourning from one place to the next, there are many moments when we reach the end of ourselves. Our patience wears thin, our willpower is low on battery, and our willingness to draw near to God in all circumstances fades into the shadows of our swelling pride.

Oftentimes, in these circumstances, we either don't know what to pray, or we find ourselves repeating the same empty phrases over and over again. It's our hope that you take these prayers and make them your own. Keep in mind, we are limited human beings and cannot out-write our own experience. You might feel some of the prayers in this book have thoughts, feelings, and/or emotions left to be said. We hope you feel the freedom to add or subtract from these prayers. If you start reading and the Spirit leads you to go "off script," follow His leading—not ours!

You may need to make some adjustments as you read. We want to make reading and praying with this book as personal as possible, so you'll notice we go back and forth between using singular and plural pronouns. Depending on how you're praying—whether it be for yourself, with a group, or on behalf of someone else—we encourage you to make the necessary changes to pronouns or insert a name, in order to make the prayer more personal to you.

Throughout the book, you'll notice pages dedicated to breath prayers. This form of prayer engages your body and mind as you meditate on one or two lines of Scripture. You simply inhale slowly and deeply while whispering the first line of prayer, then slowly exhale as you whisper the second line. Repeat the prayer as many times as you need. Henri Nouwen said of breath prayers, "This way of simple prayer, when we are faithful to it and practice it at regular times, slowly leads us to an experience of rest and opens us to God's active presence."[1]

We want to elevate God's Word above our own words. We need the Scriptures to inform and direct our prayers and to give us a renewed passion to take our requests to the throne of God. For each prayer, we've included a scripture reference and we encourage you to turn to the scripture passage for further reading.

---

1 Henri Nouwen, *The Way of the Heart*, Ballantine Books; Reissue edition (12 July 1985)

FOR THE SOJOURNER

For the displaced,
who has been forced to leave their home
due to violence, conflict,
war, or natural disaster—
give them a place to find rest and peace.
During a time of uncertainty
as to when they'll get to return
to their community,
grant them a profound and
palpable sense of communion
with You, O Lord.

For the refugee,
who has been forced to leave their nation
and sleep in crowded camps—
draw near, O Lord, to their suffering.
Bring a person of peace into their life,
who will serve them a hot meal,
and give them clean clothes to wear.
They know not how long they'll be away,
or how long until the fighting will cease.
Help them to find refuge
with You, O Lord.

For the migrant,
who has chosen to leave their country
to seek better opportunities for their life—
be a light unto their path
and lead them to the next right thing.
Provide them their basic needs:
an honest day's work,

a roof over their head,
and a meal for each day.
May they find all they're searching for
in You, O Lord.

For the immigrant,
who has moved to another country
due to work, marriage,
or to provide for a loved one—
grant them favor in the eyes of those
who handle their visa documents.
Give them peace about their future,
and mercies for each day.
Help them to know that their life
is not controlled by immigration, but
by You, O Lord.

For the asylum seeker,
who is searching for another place to live
to escape persecution of some form—
deliver them from their oppressor and
build Your hedge of protection
around their life.
Guide them to safety
and help them find their refuge and salvation
in You, O Lord.

For the stateless person,
who no longer has a country,
or whose country discriminates against
their race of people within its borders—
lift their faces to the heavens
and fill their hearts
with Your unconditional love.

Help them to believe that
the value of their life is not determined
by the status of their citizenship
here on this earth.
Rather, their value comes from belonging
to You, O Lord.

For the visitor,
who has willingly left their own country
to reside in another—
help them to enter foreign borders
with a humble heart and a learning spirit.
When they are still learning
the language and culture,
and their weaknesses are on full display,
may they draw from Your deep reservoir
of strength and grace
to carry them through each day.
And may they find comfort and familiarity
in You, O Lord.

Leviticus 19:34

INHALE

With a sincere heart

EXHALE

I draw near to You

FOR PACKING

O Lord, as the boxes and bins
lay open before me,
asking me to decide what should go
and what should stay
(an impossible question)
my heart is torn by the grief of the leaving
and the joy of the going.
Would You empty my soul of these things
that are much too heavy to hold?
For Your yoke is easy and Your burden is light.

Father, let these suitcases be altars
where I acknowledge my dependence on material things
and where I surrender to You those affections
that threaten my peace.
Forgive me for holding too tightly
to that which You've asked me to let go of.
In Your kindness, unravel their ties
around my heart,
so that my going might be in joyful freedom,
rather than reluctant obligation.

As I check and re-check the lists
and weigh and re-weigh the bags,
remind me that I will inevitably pack
something I don't need
and forget something I do.
Yet, You will sustain and uphold me,
because those who trust in You
lack no good thing.

When the last bag is packed and weighed
and the job is done,
may I find peace in knowing
You are really all I need.
For it is not what is in these containers
that make a life,
but rather, abiding in You.
And it is not what is in these containers
that give comfort,
but rather, the Comforter Himself.

The Comforter who
needs no duct tape number
or itemized list attached,
but who is ever before,
ever behind,
and ever with me,
here in this moment
and to the ends of the earth.

Matthew 6:19-20a

FOR AN INTERNATIONAL MOVE

All-Knowing God,
the One who sees where this path leads,
we are stepping out in faith.

We feel a mix of excitement for what lies ahead,
and worry about all we don't yet know.
We are moving to a new land,
learning how to live
in a new environment,
growing again
from a new beginning.

We are packing boxes and crates
and filling containers with our memories.
Goodbyes are rolling like waves,
and tears fall like rain.
Smiles and words of encouragement
shine on us like the sun.
Help us to treasure
all of these moments.

As we pack suitcases,
kiss our loved ones,
and wave last goodbyes—
steady our hearts.
As we travel, grant us safety.

Once we take our first steps in our new home,
steady us.
We will need the strength You give us.
When the frustration of registration,
cultural navigation,

and shopping wear us down—
give us rest.

Remind us
that it is important to breathe.
Remind us
that You are already there.
When we feel overwhelmed,
pour Your peace into our spirits.

We trust You,
because You know what lies ahead.
You are near,
You are dependable,
and You are the foundation we build on.
Give us opportunities to grow our roots.
In this new soil,
plant seeds of friendship and support
around us.

May we become beloved members
of our new community.

When we feel alone,
open our eyes to the slow work
of settling in.

Teach us to savor new discoveries.
Give us patience, where there is struggling.

Make us a blessing.
You are good,
and You will keep us
wherever we are.

Job 31:4

FOR TRAVEL BY PLANE

Maker of the earth and skies,
Calmer of the wind and waves—
make my heart steadfast,
and calm my anxious mind
as I embark on a journey
through the air,
above this spinning globe
of dust and dirt
that I call "home"
and You call "held."

Father, as I settle into my seat,
let Your presence settle into my heart.
As I buckle my seatbelt,
wrap Your arms around me.
As I watch the safety demonstrations,
remind me there is nowhere safer
than in Your hands,
and Your hands will not let go
of me.

Holy Spirit,
let every bump of turbulence
remind me that
You move like the wind,
to and fro over the earth—
ever with me,
ever around me.
And even when I can't see You,
I can feel You.

In these moments of
in between—
between the leaving and arriving—
may I find space to breathe deep,
to exhale stress I've been carrying,
and to inhale mercy You are extending.
Holy God,
help me find You even here,
above the clouds.
For there is nowhere I can go
that You are not there with me.

Bless me with sleep, O Jesus—
a deep, peaceful sleep.
Comfort me with rest,
so that I might reach my destination
refreshed
and ready
for what waits for me on the other side—
those good things
You've prepared in advance
for me to do.

Sovereign God,
I center my thoughts on You,
I release my anxiety to You,
I find my hope in You.

You are the One who sees the sparrow in flight,
who is watching me take flight,
who covers me with Your wings,
and who leads my feet safely
to the ground again.

Matthew 10:29-31

FOR THOSE SETTLING IN

O God of the unsettled—
I am torn,
my heart divided between
here and there.
I walk the streets
lonely and looking for comfort.
I look around
and life there goes on without me,
meanwhile it is passing me by where I stand.

I doubt my choices
to leave it all behind.
I long for a break in the clouds.
I need to hear familiar words
and taste flavors I know.
Some days,
everything feels so gray around me.

I have forgotten to look for Your providence.

Renew my hope.
Help me to look up and see
the colors You have put on my path.
Remind me that You envelop me.
Give me strength
and build up my heart
within me.

I trust in Your unfailing hands.
I know Your plan for me
is for my good.
I know that You are the map

to all I have yet to discover
in this new place.

I praise You for the flowers
that will bloom from the seeds of faith
I plant and water here.
I praise You for providing growth
and opportunity.
You are the light
which breaks the darkness
and provides all I need
to thrive where I am.

2 Corinthians 5:6

FOR UNPACKING

Holy Father,
thank You that even here, I find You
in the midst of these suitcases
that beckon me to unpack them
when I'd rather rest from the journey.
So before I begin the task,
would You help me pause in this moment
to unpack my soul first
and empty out all that is
weighing me down?

The physical journey
may have ended,
but the greater journey
is just beginning.

And I confess, I am already
feeling weary from the weight of
travel,
time zones,
and transition.
Help me, O Spirit,
to release this heaviness to You
and find comfort in Your presence.

In this holy unpacking,
reveal my hidden sin,
and cover me with Your mercy.
Expose lies I've believed,
and replace them with Your truth.
Empty out my selfish pride,

and fill me with humility.
Strip away my self-sufficiency,
and replace my weakness with Your strength.

With each suitcase I unpack
and each item I hold,
may my heart be filled with gratitude
for Your abundant provision.
Comfort me in moments when
I grieve the things left behind.
Help me hold it all loosely
so I can receive with open hands
that which You have for me here.

When the last bag is emptied
and everything put away in its new place,
let my exhale be deep,
my mind be at rest,
and my heart be at peace.
For I can find joy in knowing that
wherever I unpack my bags
and set up a home—
whether for a moment
or a lifetime,
my true home is with You
and You are ever with me.

Psalm 139:3-5

FOR REBUILDING

Builder God,

I am starting anew.
I am scared of the unknowns,
and overwhelmed by too many choices.

I feel disconnected from where I have been,
and I am unsure of what the coming days hold.

But You.

You build,
create,
dismantle,
and rebuild.

Build me a home
where You have called me.

I need Your expertise,
wisdom,
and guidance.

Amen

Psalm 127, 1 Peter 2:5

INHALE

When I feel scared
or in the dark

EXHALE

Remind me I am in the shadow
of Your wings

FOR MOVING (AGAIN)

We take a moment to pause,
to breathe in deeply,
and observe these walls that became a home.
We behold the abundant grace
You have poured into this dwelling place,
O Lord.

Soon, the disassembling will begin.
The shelves will be emptied,
the cabinets will be cleared,
the walls will be bare.

Then, the memories will flood in.
Lost toys will be found,
pictures will be rediscovered,
souvenirs will be dusted off.

We know this was always meant
to be temporary,
but we still grieve the loss
of this place being called our home.
We grieve this life
of holding something close
only to have to one day let it go.

Help us remember
that Your presence follows us,
and fullness of joy is with us
wherever we go.
This setting up and breaking down of tents
will ultimately lead us to our forever home
with You.

For now, we feel unsettled,
floating between a home that once was,
and a home that is yet to be.
And so our souls are like this, too—
dwelling here, tethered to these earthly vessels,
but always looking onward
to our eternal home.

As we look around this empty space,
we thank You for the memories
we carry with us—
the laughter,
the prayers,
the tears,
the growth,
the shared meals,
and the fellowship.

We praise You, O Lord,
for all the ways You have shaped us
while in this place.

And as we move to the next location,
help us to hold onto this truth–
just as You prepared this place for us,
we trust You'll do it again
for the next temporary dwelling
we will eventually call home.

Genesis 28:15

FOR LANGUAGE LEARNING

What a gift, O Lord,
to be able to speak to You,
with words from our heart.
You listen to and understand them all.

How redemptive, O God,
that You turned the sinful ambitions of mankind
into a multitude of languages.
You used it to scatter us, so we might be fruitful
and multiply and fill Your earth.

How wonderful, O Lord, are Your plans,
how beautiful is Your creation
and the diversity of language.
We thank You for Your promise
that all tribes, tongues, and nations
will one day gather at Your throne,
singing praises to You,
the Most High God.

Sustain us in our language learning journey.
Help us to speak the language
of the people among whom we dwell,
so that we might grow closer
in our relationships with others.

Give us the posture of humility,
as we ask for help
and seek to understand.
May we die to self and realize
our complete dependence on You.

Prepare our hearts and minds
for the opportunities we have

to practice speaking another language.
Uproot any arrogance or insecurity
that might hinder the conversation.

May we remember to rejoice
in the small victories,
and not lose heart
when we make mistakes.

And as we become more fluent,
may we never forget the importance
of being slow to speak.
May our language acquisition not simply be
for the purpose of others
being able to understand us, but also,
so that we might understand others.

Help us in our pursuit to
listen to,
converse with,
learn from,
and understand
one another.

What a gift, O Lord,
to be able to learn to speak to others
with words from our heart.
Whether we speak fluently
or fumble through our sentences,
may our words always
build others up,
uplift and edify,
and draw people closer to You—
the God of all languages.

Exodus 4:10-12, Colossians 4:5-6

FOR CROSS-CULTURAL NEIGHBORING

Sovereign God,
I know it is by Your grand design
I am here
in this house,
this community,
this country,
surrounded by these precious gifts from You,
packaged in flesh and bone:
my neighbors.

Lord, in this foreign place I am finding
I need to unlearn and relearn
how to be a good neighbor.
For we are different, they and I—
different cultures, different languages.
And I confess, I don't always know
how to bridge that gap.
Would You teach me how to love my neighbor
as myself,
even when they are not
like myself?

Creator God, help me to see
the Imago Dei
in the faces of the people I am living among,
to hear Your voice in the language they speak,
to taste Your goodness in the flavors they love,
to see Your fingerprints in the art they create.

For as I welcome them,
I welcome You,

and as I learn more of their hearts,
I see more of Yours.

Teach me the ministry of neighboring—
of being present,
available,
willing.
Help me not to use my home to
keep the world out,
but to invite them in—
expecting nothing in return,
as you, Jesus, always invite me in,
even when I have nothing to offer
except my brokenness.

Oh Lord, expand my heart—
I offer it humbly to You.
Fill it with Your love
so that strangers would become neighbors,
neighbors would become friends,
and friends would become family—
both in flesh and in spirit,
for our days here
and for all eternity.

Galatians 5:14

WHEN THE NEIGHBORS ARE LOUD

O Lord,
my soul is not at peace
and anger rages within me.

The neighbors are being
unnervingly loud
and the noise is invading my home
and encroaching on my peace.

The noise drones on and on
and I never know
when it will be finished
or when it will start up again.

O Lord, my God,
I can't fully relax in my own home
and the abrasive noise is
leaving me anxious
and restless.

You say,
love your neighbor—
but loving them seems an
impossible task to do.

You say,
do not seek revenge—
but I'm filled with so many
unpleasant emotions.

I have prayed in faith
that the noise would cease,
knowing nothing is out of Your control.

But the noise continues on,
and my soul is distressed.
How long, O Lord,
do I have to endure this?
How long, O Lord,
will my life,
my prayers,
my work,
and my sleep,
be disrupted by the perpetual noise
of my neighbors?

It saps me of my strength
and my weakness is on full display.
There's no good thought left in me
and I am prone to act out in sin.
But You, O Lord, are my refuge.
You are my present help in time of need.
Peace is available to me in this moment,
through You.

You know my anxious thoughts,
and You see my troubled soul.
Surely You are not distant from me
and Your peace is not dependent
on my circumstances.

Though I see no resolution,
I trust You will resolve what matters most.

Though I see no way to redeem this time,
I trust You will reveal a way.

In my own strength,
I'm unable to love my neighbor right now.
But in You,
I can do what currently feels impossible.

I admit, I deeply desire
for the loud noises to come to an end.
But even if the noise persists,
I know You can still bring peace
in my life,
and my soul can find rest
in You.

2 Thessalonians 3:16

INHALE

The seed I sow with tears

EXHALE

Will be harvested with joy

FOR A CULTURALLY IMMERSED DAY

As this day begins,
I pause to be still before You,
O Lord,
to center myself in Your presence
in preparation for a day of
cultural immersion
that will inevitably stretch me
and remind me that I'm forever the foreigner.
So here in this moment,
let me soak in Your presence
where I'm forever Your child.

Christ, have mercy on me
and grant me strength to navigate
cultural dilemmas with grace,
language barriers with love,
unfamiliar situations with joy,
new foods with courage,
and unknown expectations with humility.

Give me a holy burden
for the people I will interact with,
that I might be a vessel of Your love.
Remind me that
they are created in Your image
and I love You best when
I love Your people well,
even when I may not understand
all they do.

Lord, I confess,
I often prefer my own culture
over that of others.
But the truth is,
there is no culture that is holy
and all cultures reflect pieces of You,
as a shattered mirror reflects
a broken image of something whole.

Help me in my brokenness to
love others in theirs.
Help me see You
in them,
help them see You
in me.

At the end of this day
when my mind and body are
exhausted from the work of
being immersed in this foreign experience,
let my heart be filled with
gratitude
for the gift of this life
and this culture that so beautifully
displays the creativity and character
of the One who made it all.

Psalm 5:3

FOR CULTURE FATIGUE

O Lord, today I come
crawling before Your throne,
weary and worn
from the exhaustion of living
in a culture different from my own.
I confess,
there are things about this place
You've called me to
that seem to drain every ounce
of grace and mercy out of me.
I thank You
for Your mercies that are new every morning—
I have surely used them all up for today.

Father, this culture fatigue
is heavy.
I can feel it in my bones and nerves,
I can hear it in the shortness of the words I speak,
I can see it in my lack of grace and energy.
Holy God, meet me here.
Let Your Spirit breathe renewed life
into my tired soul,
as I take this moment
to mentally step out of the culture around me
and into Your presence.

Forgive me, God, for the times when
I think my way is better
than the way of my host culture.
For as I am created in Your image,
so are they.

And as they are flawed by sin,
so am I.
May this common ground
of spirit and struggle and sin
always bind my heart to theirs.
In the times of both wonder and fatigue,
remind me that culture is simply
a vessel
where Your image can be displayed
and not the sum of our identity.
Our identity is found in You.

Merciful Jesus,
You so beautifully showed
what it looks like
to be in culture but not of it—
to celebrate culture while rejecting sin,
to transform culture through radical sacrifice.
You ministered within a culture
and yet transcended it.
Teach me what it looks like
to love this culture,
to love these people,
while also longing for it, for them,
to be redeemed.

And when my mind, my heart,
my body, and my soul
grow tired again of existing outside
of the culture most familiar to me
(because this won't be the last time)
would You give me the wisdom and grace,
O Lord,
to stop,

to step away,
to get alone with You?
For the solace I'm seeking isn't found
in my own home culture,
but in You.
The rest I am needing
is not bound by geography,
but is found in the culture of Your Kingdom come,
here within me
in this foreign land,
and wherever I am in the world.

Galatians 6:9

INHALE

You satisfy

EXHALE

My every longing

FOR CULTURE SHOCK

Lord, my banner,
as I walk these streets
and stare at unfamiliar words and letters,

I am overwhelmed.

When I look for familiar things in the store,
it sometimes stops me dead in my tracks.

How can it be that such simple things
are suddenly so complicated?

People move differently,
eat weird food,
and express things in ways I don't recognize.

Help me to remember—
even in foreign places,
You are my banner.

I am still here
and I can be recognized
as Yours
through the love and kindness I give.

Remind me that—
every day won't feel this hard
and over time it will all get better.

With all of the changes around me,
You remain the same.

Thank You for showing me new sides of Your presence as I discover You along the streets of my new home.

Hebrews 6:17

MAKING A CULTURAL MISTAKE

Merciful Lord,
compassionate, kind, and unchanging,

I am embarrassed.
It feels at times that I am a lost child.

I am beating myself up
over a cultural misunderstanding.

My mistake might have caused another pain
and I'm not sure if my words were right or wrong.

I have a sinking feeling
what I said was not appropriate.

But by the time I realized it,
things had moved on.

I feel stuck.

A mix of emotions
are coursing through me.
I want to give up and hide away.

Remind me that I can grow through this.
Comfort my heart.

Help me to know what to do now.
I need Your guidance.

Teach me to be kind to myself
and seek peace.

Your thoughts toward me are full of grace.
Help me learn to be gracious to myself
and remember tomorrow is a new day.

If I have caused another hurt or frustration,
comfort them.

Give me an opportunity
to restore the relationship,
and wisdom to know how to do it.

If I simply misinterpreted what happened,
and the person is not fazed,
calm my heart
and restore peace to my soul.

Psalm 86:3-7

FOR COMPARISON

Father, I confess—
though my feet
have walked in obedience
to this foreign land,
my eyes tend to wander.

I find my gaze lingering
on the lives of others,
falling prey to comparison.
I often wonder if I am enough
and wish I could be
more,
less,
other than what I am
and where You've called me.

When I'm tempted
to compare my work,
ministry,
family,
home,
possessions,
and abilities
to those of others,
remind me that I cannot
run the race to which You've called me
if I'm too busy worrying about
everyone else's.

The sound of fluency
from others

causes me to doubt
if this language will ever
roll off my tongue with ease.

But rather than
let their ability
discourage me,
may it inspire me
to persevere, to press on,
to give You praise for their gift
and for the lives they can touch
because of it.

Be merciful to me, Holy Spirit,
and steady my heart
when it's tossed by waves of
doubt.
When I see fruit
in the lives of others,
and I wonder why the seeds I've sown
lie dormant,
remind me that
You are the One who makes
the seed grow.
You don't measure success by results,
but rather, by obedience.

Forgive me Lord,
for the discontentment
that settles heavy in my soul
when my eyes are fixed on others
rather than You.
In Your kindness,

shift my gaze upward
and help me to trust that

You are in me,
You are with me,
You are for me,
You are good.

Satisfy my heart with Your presence
so that I long for no other thing.
And let the community
You have blessed me with
be a source of fellowship,
rather than frustration.
For You have not asked me
to be like them,
but You have called me
to be like You.

And when I abandon comparison,
I can walk in surrender—
being conformed to Your likeness,
no longer wondering if
I am enough,
because I know that You are.

Galatians 5:25-26

INHALE

Your kindness and love

EXHALE

Can be found each day

FOR GROCERY SHOPPING

Creator God,
Giver of all good things—
thank You for the gift of
the fruit of the earth
that fills our bellies
with sustenance,
our souls
with comfort,
and our senses
with wonder.

For today, Lord
I marvel at all these ingredients
that are foreign to me,
the smells and flavors and textures
I see in the markets here
that are new and different and strange.
I confess that sometimes
I see more of what's missing
than of Your provision.
Would You help me
not to focus on the lack of what's familiar,
but rather, the beauty in the diversity
of Your created world?

As I study the foreign labels,
give me a heart to study Your Word.
As I search for that one ingredient,
may I search for Your truth.
As I crave the food of my childhood,
help me crave the fruit of Your Spirit.

As I count up my foreign currency,
let me count my many blessings.

Give me my daily bread,
O Bread of Life,
that I would feast on You
all of my days.
Quench my thirst,
O Living Water,
that I would drink of Your goodness
till the end of time.

As You multiplied the loaves and fish,
multiply Yourself to me.
When my cravings for
familiar foods remain
unmet,
may I remember Your invitation
to the table
You've set for me—
where every longing is fulfilled
as I taste and see that
even here,
You are good.

Matthew 6:11

FOR TERRIBLE TRAFFIC

My soul is not at peace, O Lord.
I can feel the rush of emotions—
unleashed and unfiltered,
when I try and navigate the roads
to reach my final destination.

I am agitated and restless
when the journey doesn't go as planned.
And I feel stuck in my powerlessness
to do anything about it.

Search my heart
and throw out the impatience.
Inhale May mercy, peace, and love
Exhale be multiplied to me.

Search my heart
and pull out any false illusion
that I am in control of time.
Inhale I plan my course,
Exhale but You establish my steps.

Search my heart
and remove my frustration.
Inhale Give me a spirit of love
Exhale and help me extend grace.

Remind me, O Lord,
that every day we are waiting.

We wait for answers,
we wait for healing,

we wait for justice,
we wait for the salvation of others,
we wait for Jesus to come
and take us home.

We are all on our way
to our final destination,
but we are not there yet.

Teach me to wait on You, O Lord,
as I sit in this traffic
and navigate these roads.

Help me to see the obstacles and delays
as part of Your sovereign plan
to get me where I need to be.

Develop in my heart
the difficult practice of patience
and grant my soul peace during the journey.

Proverbs 3:5-6, Proverbs 16:9

WHEN THE ELECTRICITY/WATER IS OUT

Lord, I acknowledge in this moment
the regular blessings I take for granted.
When modern conveniences
like the circulation of electricity
or water flowing through the pipes
are temporarily unavailable to me,
I immediately feel the agitation
of discomfort.

As I sit here,
suddenly without something I expected,
help me to take my thoughts captive.
Keep me, Lord, from growing frustrated,
angry, or casting blame on others
for this minor inconvenience.

In the absence of these comforts
draw me closer to You.
You are the God of all comfort.
Search my heart,
and purge it of all self-reliance.
My sufficiency comes from You, O Lord.

When modern comforts are gone,
tune my heart,
my thoughts,
my prayers,
to praise You for these blessings.
I acknowledge these things
as gifts from Your hands.

Even when these conveniences
are not available to me,
You are still good.

Even when I sit
in the darkness,
Your light still remains.

Even when the pipes
are dry and desiccated,
You are a steady stream of living water.

Reorient my heart
to sing praise
to the God who gives
and takes away.

Conveniences come and go,
but You, O Lord, remain forever.

Job 2:10 NIV

WHEN THERE ARE ANTS IN THE SUGAR

When there are ants in the sugar,
rats under the stove,
faulty wiring in the walls,
and mold in the ceiling—

Inhale whatever is true and honorable,
Exhale help me dwell on these things.

When there are gnats in the sink,
mosquitoes in the bed sheets,
larvae on the laundry,
and bats on the porch—

Inhale whatever is just and pure,
Exhale help me dwell on these things.

When there are gecko droppings in the kitchen,
bugs in the dried noodles and rice,
poor piping in the drainage system,
and rooms that regularly flood—

Inhale whatever is lovely and commendable,
Exhale help me dwell on these things.
When there are termites in the door frames,
roaches on the countertops,
smoke from burning trash,
and loud noises at inconvenient hours—

Lord, God of peace,
whenever I encounter these annoyances
and problems that can't be fixed,
use these moments

to help me dwell
on anything excellent and worthy of praise—

Inhale so Your peace
Exhale will dwell in me.

Philippians 4:8-9

FOR TAKING A WALK

God of heaven—
before my life began,
You ordained my steps
and knew that I would walk
these foreign pathways.
So today I acknowledge
Your sovereignty in these moments
and invite Your presence
to inhabit these very steps
You planned so long ago.

May the gospel of peace
cover my feet
so that everywhere I walk
might become fertile soil
for the kingdom,
and the Good News
would take root
and bear fruit
in every corner of this community
for the glory of Your name.

For every neighbor I pass,
for every shopkeeper I see,
for every child I smile at,
for every person I greet,
let Your Holy Spirit
be evident in me
and be at work in them.

Jesus, teach me
how to walk as You did—
never hurried
and always noticing
those who needed
an encounter with You.
As You walked in
humble surrender to
the Father's will,
teach me to do the same.

Today and every day
help me walk in obedience,
going wherever You would call me,
until I've taken the Good News
of Your infinite love
as far as you lead me
that You might call
these two humble feet
beautiful.

Psalm 119:35

FOR VISAS AND IMMIGRATION

O God, El Roi—
the God who sees me.
I know You see me in this moment,
consumed by the requirements
handed to me
in order to stay as a guest
in this foreign land.

I know all our days are numbered
here on this earth,
but I feel it even more so
as I count the number of days
before my permission to be in country
ticks down to zero.

I admit,
the hoops I have to jump through
often make me think,
Is it worth it?

Lord, I lay these things at Your feet—
the thick stacks of paperwork,
the photos with specific dimensions and backgrounds,
the folders that must be a certain color,
the interrogative questions,
the unwarranted suspicions of my intentions to live here,
the unnecessary waiting
while my visa application sits on a desk
next to idle hands,
the request for additional money
to be slid under the table,

and this nagging feeling that
I have very little control
over the whole process.

I confess,
I feel helpless being at the mercy
of people who might dislike me
for reasons I do not know.

Even when I take care to do
everything that is asked of me,
there always seems to be something
added onto the list
of requirements.

Is it worth it?

If I'm meant to stay here
as a guest in this foreign land,
help me to find favor in the eyes
of those looking over my paperwork.

If this is where You want me, Lord,
guide me like You did the Israelites
in the wilderness.
Be like a pillar of smoke,
and a bright flame
leading me in the right direction.

If my time here is not yet finished,
give me grace and patience.
Even if my visa paperwork is mishandled
or misplaced,
help me to respond in a way
that honors Christ.

As I stand in a line
or wait in a room
labeled with "foreigner,"
may it remind me
of my status here on earth.

We are all sojourners,
wandering from place to place
until we reach our eternal home.

In moments of waiting
for my permission to stay
or my instruction to leave,
help me remember that,
even though I am a stranger in this land,
I'm no stranger to You—
El Roi, the God who sees me.

Romans 13:1-3

INHALE

In the midst of
this chaos

EXHALE

You speak peace

FOR CLOSED BORDERS

Most Holy God,
would You extend Your great mercy
to my impatient heart?
I acknowledge today that You
are not restricted by
governments or systems or
borders
in the same way I am.
And You—
not governments or systems
or borders—
hold my future in Your hands.

King of Kings,
would You move in the hearts
of those in power?
Would You grant us favor?
Would You make a way,
O God who parts seas,
who crumbles walls,
who moves mountains,
who makes the impossible,
possible?

I confess I've struggled
to understand why
You would tie my heart to a place
that I cannot go.
Father, remind me that while I feel the
urgency of time—
time passing, time lost—

You are not bound by time or space.
Your purposes are not thwarted.
You are not in a hurry,
so I don't need to be, either.

Holy Spirit,
help me to rest in Your comfort
and find peace in knowing
that even in this season of waiting,
Your plans for me are still good.
Your will for me isn't
to be any certain place
except in Your presence.

Jesus, in my waiting,
teach me to trust Your sovereignty.
For with the same deep longing
I have to be in places
closed to me,
You desire for me
to long to be with You.
While earthly borders
may be impassible,
Your cross gives me access
to be in the one place I am always welcome—
with You.

Revelation 3:7

WHEN YOU GET TOO MUCH ATTENTION

I admit, Lord,
at times the attention
feels like more than I can handle.

I feel it bearing down—
a palpable weight
of discomfort
when I know
all eyes are on me.

I feel like an alien
when others want to
touch my hair,
feel my skin,
take my photo,
and watch my every move.

I long to fit in,
and not cause a need
for second glances.
I want to feel normal,
and not hear whispers
announcing my presence.
I want to sit,
eat,
exercise,
shop,
walk around,
and go about my business
without drawing crowds
of onlookers.

But You, O Lord,
are familiar with this attention.
There is nothing I'm experiencing
that You haven't experienced already.

You, too, walked this earth
and caused heads to turn.

You, too, had crowds
gather around You.

You, too, had people whisper,
and announce Your presence in a room.

People reached for You,
touched You,
and tugged at Your cloak.

But Your response was
always gracious.
Your eyes always saw
the image bearer.
Your heart was always motivated
to grow the Kingdom of God.

Help me to reflect Your love
with those around me—
even in my passing glances
and brief interactions.

Help me to humbly accept
that some situations
require me to feel uncomfortable
in order that I might grow and learn.

Keep my heart from desiring
to merely blend in with those around me,
and help me to embrace the ways
You've made me different.
As God's children,
we are image bearers of You—
each representing
a beautifully diverse Kingdom of God.
We are set apart.
We are different.
We are in this world,
but not of this world.
O Lord, help me to draw others to You,
not push them away.
May others see Your love through me.

Hebrews 11:13b-14

INHALE

While so many things
are changing

EXHALE

You remain the same

RESPONDING TO INJUSTICE

I come to you, Jesus,
with a heart that is heavy
and broken
by the injustice I bear witness to here,
and the helplessness I feel
to do anything about it.
I cry out to You
to relieve this suffering
and redeem this sorrow.
It feels like the world is burning,
but You make beauty from ashes.

Father God,
the brokenness is so deep,
the need, so overwhelming,
the poverty, so heartbreaking,
the injustice, so infuriating.
Sometimes I question
where You are in all of this.
Then You whisper,
"In you."

Empower me, Lord,
to be a vessel of Your hope and healing
to those who are hurting.
Lead me to the lonely,
bind me to the broken—
not for me to be a savior,
but so I might lead them to
the Savior.

Righteous Judge,
would You execute Your justice?

Let the wicked and their oppression
be exposed in Your light.
Let the innocent and oppressed
be liberated by Your love.
And may their freedom
be a testimony
of Your mighty power
that will not be
overcome by evil.

Praise be to You,
O God, who
takes what the enemy intends for
evil
and uses it for
good.
And when it seems like
evil is winning,
we remember
that it's just a facade—
because Christ already won the victory.

When the suffering around me is
too much to bear,
would You remind me that
Your yoke is easy and
Your burden is light?
Your intention isn't for me to carry this alone.
As You lead me to the broken,
You are really leading me to Yourself—
the One who will make every wrong right and
wipe every tear from our eyes—
our hope, our healing forever.

Psalm 82:2-3

FOR GETTING A MEDICAL DIAGNOSIS

All-Powerful Father,
the One who is able to do all and be all,
we are scared.

Our next steps are uncertain and
the future is beyond our grasp...

Hearing bad news in a language that doesn't connect to our hearts
makes bad news harder.

It feels cold, distant, and somehow separate.
We long for a better explanation, for understanding.
This diagnosis packs a punch on its own.

Having to translate and research before really understanding
all that is going on is defeating.

Give us clarity.
Help us to grieve as we process.

When we wait for results, or go through many tests,
may Your peace flow into our spirits.

As we watch our loved one go through hard things,
may Your strength flow between us.

As we walk this journey, Lord,
help us to see all the ways You light the path.

Remind us You are capable, near,
and that You bring healing.

May we be ever diligent in prayer and not afraid to ask for help.
Surround us with supporting hands, listening ears,
and those who will speak Your words back to us.

Give us a community to accompany our family during this time.
Although we might feel weak, powerless, or hopeless,
we know that You are not limited by our weakness or fear.

You can make all things new.
You are able to heal and reverse.
In the event that it is Your will not to do so,
may we humbly submit and trust that
You will give us all we need to survive the aftermath.
We praise You for Your limitless power.
We acknowledge that You are greater, bigger,
wise and trustworthy.
Let us not forget this when we receive a scary diagnosis.
Anything You will is effortlessly accomplished.

We praise You and honor You for being all that we need in
challenging times.

Isaiah 43:2

FOR GETTING NEWS OF A DEATH, ACCIDENT OR OTHER TRAGEDY

Compassionate Lord,
who feels and understands,
we are devastated.

It feels as though time stands still.
Something has happened, and we are in shock.

Learning of loss when we are far away hits us hard.
We struggle to process our mixed emotions.
Sadness sets in.
Guilt tries to intrude.
Grief becomes a constant, yet unpredictable companion.

Our knees buckle, and our bellies knot up.
How do we handle all of this from so far away?

We want to be with loved ones.
We need a Comforter who shares our heart language.

It is easy to say "I'm fine" in another language,
but our hearts long for more.
Sometimes we just answer that way,
because we can't find
(or don't know)
words to express our deep pain.

While we wait to travel and be near loved ones,
comfort us.
If it is not possible for us to be physically present,
give us Your peace.

You are actively seeking to love on us,
so may we feel this love in tangible ways.

You are merciful,
You are good,
and You are looking over us all.

Give us the opportunity
to share this love with others who grieve.

May we also radiate You
to those who come to gather near us
in our pain.

When we feel broken,
remind us that You bind us up.

As we search for answers,
may we find Your constant nature.
Give us understanding,
and remind us to trust who You are.

Hold us near.

We give You the glory in all things.
Anything You will is effortlessly accomplished.
We praise You and honor You
for being all that we need in challenging times.

1 Peter 5:7

WHEN A BIG DECISION NEEDS TO BE MADE

Sovereign God, ruler of all things,
I am facing a big decision
and I struggle to stand up
under the weight of it.
I need Your wisdom and guidance.

My desire is to do the thing
that brings honor to You.
Show me where You are leading me,
that I may join in where You are already at work.

Help me to see past my selfish needs and desires.
Unite my mind with Yours
and give me peace.

Help me to remember
that wisdom begins with You.
You counsel me
and give me understanding.
Help me to quiet the noise within
so I can hear Your guiding voice.

Enable me to see and pay attention
to all the ways You whisper Your will
in this situation.

You are light—
make visible my path forward.
Grow me in this process.
Refine me,
and make me look more like You.

I trust You
and put my confidence in You.
No matter what decision I make,
I am confident You will be there.

Psalm 86:11

FOR ELECTIONS (IN PASSPORT COUNTRY)

Omnipresent Lord,
the God who is at hand,
remind us that You are everywhere.

Even when we are far away, You are not.
Justice,
peace,
and righteousness
are Your concern.

At times it is overwhelming to be a foreigner.
Our concern is for good things to be done—
both where we are,
and where we have been.

Our neighbors view us as representatives
of where we come from.
When they don't understand what is going on,
we are questioned.

Teach us to measure our words
and answer lovingly.
Our actions and words reveal things
about our hearts.
Keep them centered on Your truth,
not political preferences.

As we vote from afar,
help us to respect the privilege to do so,
and to prayerfully consider it.

When we don't understand what we see from a distance,
teach us to speak kindly of our passport country
and remember our loved ones with grace.

Above all, turn the hearts of men toward Your will
of justice and love.
Raise up candidates
who bow their knees to you.
Give us leaders
who choose humility over pride.

You are the One who brings judgment
and deals in fairness to all You created.
Even when we can't see or recognize
the ways You are at work in the background,
remind us this world is not our home.
Teach us how to model it after Your ideals,
while we wait for You.

John 13:34-35, Romans 13:10, Galatians 5:14

FOR ELECTIONS (IN HOST COUNTRY)

Omnipotent Father,
You who holds all things together.

We are living through a local election.
Decisions will be made that may impact us.
While living here as foreigners,
we can't choose the outcome.
Still, we care about the results.

Guide those seeking to lead.
May they show kindness to those like us
building a home in their homeland.

Allow our neighbors a moment
of clarity and reflection.
Help them to be discerning.

Where peace is absent, send it.
Where compassion is needed, soften hearts.
Where kindness is lacking,
and basic needs remain unmet,
Lord, make a way.

Regardless of the outcome,
remind us that You are our provider,
establisher of all things,
who holds all things together.

Proverbs 2:6, Colossians 3:13-14

INHALE

You make a way

EXHALE

Where there is no way

FOR LOSS OF FRIENDSHIPS

Loving Father,
making a home
far from the home I have known
is lonely.
Some days,
I have no meaningful interactions
outside of my family.
I miss my old friends,
I long for new ones.

Making friends
in a different country
means I have to learn new rules.
Learning takes time and
loneliness fills the space
that time creates.

Open my eyes
to the moments of progress.
Help me see opportunities
to build relationships.

Even when I can't see
how it will turn out,
I know that You don't want
for me to be alone.

I praise You for Your heart
for relationships.
I praise You that You created us
to need and long for fellowship.
I trust You to lead me

to a new community
because You are a God
of community.

Psalm 147:3

FOR MISSING 'HOME'

O God who is near,
we know You are always with us, and yet,
our hearts often feel the ache
of homesickness.

O God our shelter,
we know these tents we dwell in are temporary, and yet
we can't help but long for
certain corners of this earth.

Though this world is not our home,
we still experience joy and fellowship
within the walls and under the shelter
of structures built by man.

Though this world is not our home,
we still find a sense of belonging
when we are in the company of those
who are like-minded and of kindred spirit.

We recognize these moments
of peaceful habitation,
of secure dwellings,
of quiet rest,
as the work of Your hands, Lord.

We praise You for giving us
these glimpses of heaven.
And we look forward to the day
when we'll no longer be separated
from the ones we love.

We find comfort in knowing our hearts
will not always ache
for all the places we call home.

Remind us, O Lord–
in these moments when we long to be
where we belong–
our eternal dwelling is in heaven
and our belonging is found in You.

Remind us, O Lord–
in these moments when we feel unsettled—
we dwell in the shelter of the Most High
and abide in the shadow of the Almighty.

May our homesickness remind us
to chase after things eternal.
May it constantly point our eyes upward
to our heavenly dwelling,
and outward
to the ones we desire to join us there.

Turn our heartache for homes here on earth
into a longing to be home with You—
where we'll surely find our secure dwelling
and our quiet rest.

2 Corinthians 5:1

LIVING WHERE YOU DON'T FULLY BELONG

Lord of belonging, remind us that we are wanted.

We feel like outsiders—
always just on the edge of all that is happening,
longing to feel a part of the community,
mourning the tiny ways we feel more disconnected from
where we come from,
experiencing guilt for missing familiar things and enjoying new
favorites.

We struggle to deeply express our emotions
in a language not our own.
Lonely days leave us feeling disconnected.
Holidays are bittersweet.
We miss familiarity, while learning new traditions and flavors.

When we find ourselves alone in a crowd,
remind us that we are seen.
In times we are misunderstood,
help us to feel Your comfort.
After hours, days, weeks, and years of pouring ourselves out,
it is often hard not to participate in self-pity,
because we feel so empty.

Remind us You are constant.
Help us not to give up—
give us strength to follow Your lead.
Renew our energy and give us clear minds,
ready to continue to do the work of living as strangers.

Though we feel weary, we trust You.
You sustain us,

You don't abandon us.
You teach us through this life all the varied ways You love.
Remind us that our lives are meant to do the same.

We praise You for allowing us the unique opportunity
to witness just how wide and deep Your love for all mankind is.
You are good, caring, and consistent.
Your name be praised.

Matthew 11:28-30

BENEDICTION

May we, as sojourners on this dusty sphere, have eyes to see the image of the Creator in every tribe, tongue, and nation He has created. As we traverse countries and continents, may we walk in humility, recognizing that we have much to learn of God and the world He has made.

May our steps and daily actions leave behind the footprints of God. May our eyes see as He does, while our hands are quick to share and comfort.

May our journey be blessed, as unpredictable as it often seems. May we be ever aware of God's movements and strong enough to join Him where He is busy. May we resist the temptation to put our will above the Lord's.

May we seek to live in harmony with others and outdo one another in being helpful and kind. Though our lives often feel like a revolving door of people coming and going, may our hearts be rooted in the Word of God so that Christ's love would overflow from our lives and into the lives of our neighbors.

May our attempts to learn a new language also teach us to be slow to speak and quick to listen—not simply because we lack the vocabulary, but because we desire to understand. In this world, there's no shortage of "humble opinions." May we be a people who truly humble ourselves, having the heart of a learner, knowing that every good conversation begins with good listening.

May we learn to navigate, speak, and live in a new land, but also recognize the ways God works and moves differently in the places we find ourselves. May we never forget that though He is ONE God, He shares Himself with His creation in innumerable ways.

May every ache for home and belonging ever lead us to the hope of an eternal dwelling place Jesus is preparing for us. While we remain on this earth, may we always travel light, remembering that our treasure is not found in suitcases and storage bins, but in heaven.

May our hearts align with God's heart to act justly, love mercy, and walk humbly with Him all the days of our lives.

Amen

AFTERWORD

You're holding this book in your hands right now and we're here to tell you—it's no coincidence.

Just like it was no coincidence how the beginning of this book started in the hearts of three women, in three different countries, who were each blissfully unaware of one another's plans to write prayers for fellow sojourners.

Part of this book's story began in the mountains of Laos.

Another part of this book's story began in a Starbucks in Indonesia.

And a third part of the story began as a middle-of-the-night prayer in Austria.

This is how God works, friends. There are no coincidences—only His all-knowing hand guiding us from one moment to the next. He is not bound by borders, time zones, languages, or visa stamps. This book is a testimony to how He is both intimately involved in each of our lives, yet bigger than this globe we temporarily call home.

Because this is one of our favorite stories, we'd like to take a moment to share how the three of us came together to work on this first volume of *Liturgies and Laments for the Sojourner*. There's no denying how God was in every detail, from beginning to end.

Heather's Story

I wasn't raised in a liturgical church, and knew nothing of liturgy until my young adult years. My teeth were cut on the pews of churches where pastors prayed with emotional fervor and congregants responded with passionate, vocal affirmations. Hearing prayers offered with confidence from saints who truly believed we can, "come boldly to the throne of grace..." (Heb. 4:16) formed my theology of prayer.

When I first attended a service framed by liturgy, I wasn't sure how to respond. Was prayer as meaningful if the words weren't birthed from my own mind and heart? Could prayers read from a page hold as much power as spontaneous ones?

In 2015, our family's transition overseas and immersion into foreign language and culture left me feeling tongue-tied. I experienced so many things I didn't have words to process, but my heart desperately needed to be unburdened at the feet of the Father. Words failed me, so I turned to the book of Psalms. I saw myself in David's prayers, and I processed the emotion I didn't have words to express as I prayed with the psalmist. I discovered prayers read from a page can hold great power, but the power isn't in the written words. It's in the heart-posture of the one praying.

I found that my inner life was enriched by prayers written by others who had experienced holy encounters with God in similar seasons. Through their words, my emotions were illuminated and given space to be brought into communion with Christ. I began to write prayers of my own, words reflecting my desperation for Jesus to meet me on this foreign soil. Something stirred in me as I realized my love for the written word and for fellowship with the Father could perhaps be a blessing to others who were also struggling to find language to express the complexities of life abroad in prayer.

When I listened to a podcast interview in March 2021 with Douglas Kaine McKelvey, the author of *Every Moment Holy*, I felt a nudge from the Spirit. People loved his prayers which recognized the liturgy in the everyday, but what about those of us whose everyday looks rather...unusual? What about the wanderer, the traveler, the foreigner making a home in a distant land? Where were the prayers for our unique circumstances and situations? They didn't exist.

So, with trembling hands and heart, I created @liturgiesforalifeabroad on Instagram. Not being a well-known social media presence, I didn't have high expectations for the account. I simply wanted to be obedient to what I felt the Father asking me to do. Since then, I have been amazed at the response. Time and time again, reader's comments and messages have confirmed the need for prayers like these, and I've felt incredibly humbled to be a part of filling that gap.

Alicia's Story

The longing for a book like this one started when I was mentally exhausted from communicating in another language. It continued when I felt anything *but* love for my noisy neighbors. It hung in the air and echoed off the walls of yet another empty house we would need to turn into a home.

In these moments, I often didn't know what to pray. The words came up short and I usually turned to a psalm and let the verses intercede on my behalf. And while God's Word is completely sufficient and more than enough for this purpose, a thought constantly bounced around in my head: *wouldn't it be nice to have a book of prayers specifically for foreigners living outside their home country?*

Here's something you should know about me: I write stories, not prayers. I tell things in narrative, not poetically. Never once did I consider myself for the job of writing a book of prayers for foreigners. But in March 2021, I could no longer deny the Holy Spirit's nudge I continued to feel each time I thought about the book idea.

One particular afternoon, I sat in Starbucks and stared at the cursor blinking at the end of my first written liturgy. If I wanted this book, I would need to write it.

So I said yes—albeit, very hesitantly—and realized I had a lot of work ahead of me if I was going to write a whole book of prayers. For accountability, I decided to start sharing the book idea with a few close friends. But beyond those few people, no one knew I had a book in the works.

A few weeks later, while I was on a beach vacation with my family, I got a friend request on Instagram from an account called @liturgiesforalifeabroad. *Wait, what? How? Who?* I couldn't believe it. Someone else had the same idea as me, but for Instagram. And it wasn't just some random person on the internet—it was Heather, a fellow writer friend of mine.

To be fully transparent with you all, my heart sank a little bit in that moment. I couldn't write a book with the exact same purpose and vision as my friend's new Instagram account. I felt happy for Heather, knowing she would do a great job writing these prayers. I also felt sadness about a project I had finally said yes to, only to have to let it go a few weeks later.

I spent the next several days wondering why God had nudged me so much about that book idea. Maybe it was all a lesson in obedience. Maybe it was a lesson in trusting God, even when I didn't feel like I was the right person for the job. Even if the book didn't happen, He was still a good God for nudging me to take steps in that direction.

But the nudges didn't seem to stop. Try as I might to move on with my life, I could not stop thinking about the book. Finally, God planted a thought right into my head: *What if I ask Heather if she's interested in working on the book together?*

I drafted a message in WhatsApp, paced around my house, did mental somersaults back and forth about whether or not to extend the invitation, and finally pressed send. I could barely look at my phone afterward, agonizing over what would happen next. But lo and behold, she responded with an enthusiastic yes. I exhaled the breath I had been holding and the book dream was brought back to life. Onward!

But God still had some nudging left to do. Quietly at first, but more persistently as time went on, God brought Tamika's name to my mind. I had seen Tamika write beautiful posts on Instagram and share liturgies and laments written by others, but I had no idea if she was interested in writing prayers—let alone, joining a book project. Cue me pacing the house again and continually putting off extending the invitation.

Then one morning, while brushing my teeth, Tamika's name came to my mind so suddenly, I could have sworn I heard her name said aloud. I went straight from the bathroom to my laptop and typed up an email with the subject line, "An Invitation to Join a Project."

I whispered a prayer, clicked send, and listened to the *whoosh* sound as my email went on its way to an inbox in Austria.

Tamika's Story

The opportunity to be a part of this came to me when I was at the lowest point I ever remember being spiritually. I felt a loneliness that left me gasping for air most days. It goes without saying, but living as a foreigner can be really isolating. It feels like sitting in the desert staring at a mirage some days—the illusion of what you thirst for is just beyond reach. I was thirsting for community and people who could relate to my experience.

I began posting only black and white images on my Instagram and telling stories of my genealogy searches. Privately, I was writing laments for people who were experiencing loss. I would send the messages as DMs or texts when I felt prompted by the Lord, and discovered this was a beautiful new form of worship. The act of noticing God had settled in next to me in my grief.

I felt called to let Him speak through me to others sitting in the shadows of life. The question remained: *how would I do this?* Would I just continue sending messages? Or was there a different way?

I had been listening to a lesson about David—a man of spiritual practice who approached God in all situations. He also wrote prayers. In the story of David and Goliath, I was interested to learn what was pushing David to have courage. It was his desire to *Kiddush HaShem* (in Hebrew: משה שודיק). It means "sanctification of the Name," to keep the name and reputation of the Lord clean. My soul longed to do the same.

One source of my grief was feeling troubled and burdened about the spiritually displaced. I am passionate about others knowing that God will join them wherever they find themselves— no matter the circumstances, or emotional state. So I wrote prayers of lament. But I wasn't confident that it was time for me to do anything with the prayers.

During the lesson about David, I was reminded that it wasn't about what I did with the prayers. They were to be an offering. I simply needed to listen for the promptings of the Spirit and see what God would do with the prayers. Just like the stones David had, the first step was to throw them—what happened next was God's business. Not long after, I had an email from Alicia inviting me to join this project. I threw my stone.

Though we have never been in the same place in real life, these girls have become treasures to me. We met via Zoom to brainstorm. We used Google and WhatsApp to plan and communicate. Because I am behind Alicia and Heather in time, I often woke up to several messages in our group chat. They would wake up and make suggestions and edits, and I would format the book while they were sleeping. This became a regular rhythm of the writing and editing process.

I have most enjoyed seeing how varied our own experiences are. I juggle three cultures in my own life in Europe, and they each live in two different cultures in Southeast Asia. I don't always relate to some of the things they experience and vice versa. I believe this has added depth to our writing that might not have been there if we all lived in the same place.

In his book, *Every Moment Holy*[2], Douglas Kaine McKelvey wrote "A Liturgy for the Writing of Liturgies." The prayer starts off by saying, "How fearful a vocation is the writing of liturgies, O Lord, for it presumes the shaping of words that others will speak to You."

As we sat down to write these prayers, we were acutely aware of the responsibility we were holding and our need to make space in our hearts, souls, and minds for God to fill. We needed to hear from Him and hold His words in our hearts so we could be vessels worthy of this task He had called us to do.

We've had to be honest with ourselves and embrace a posture of prayerful dependence on God before engaging in the holy work of writing liturgical prayers and laments for fellow sojourners. We all bring experiences that shape how we perceive things—but when we acknowledge where we are and invite God to search our hearts, we are better able to be led by Him.

---

2 *Every Moment Holy* by Douglas McKelvey (2017, Hardcover) published by Rabbit Room

Some of these prayers were written with the clarity of hindsight, while other prayers were written in the thick of it. It is our hope and desire that our striving to arrange words just so might be stirred to life by God within each individual and turn countless hearts toward Jesus. We hope these prayers will serve as a burst of wind in your sails that ushers you into a place of communion with God—where you are most certainly loved, remembered, known, and seen.

Made in the USA
Las Vegas, NV
16 September 2023

77663619R00059